SONNET

for
Mum and Dad

Christopher Knight

AuthorHouse™ UK
1663 Liberty Drive
Bloomington, IN 47403 USA
www.authorhouse.co.uk
UK TFN: 0800 0148641 (Toll Free inside the UK)
UK Local: 02036 956322 (+44 20 3695 6322 from outside the UK)

This book is printed on acid-free paper.

ISBN: 978-1-6655-9943-6 (sc)
ISBN: 978-1-6655-9942-9 (e)

Library of Congress Control Number: 2022911321

Print information available on the last page.

Published by AuthorHouse 07/21/2022

authorHOUSE®

Sonnet for Mum and Dad

Christopher Knight

BOOK I

Alfie and Malty

Alfie and Malty

Alfie, Malty, what are we going to do?
Alfie, Malty, do you see that cat looking at you?
Too late, Malty—the cat has jumped away.
Alfie and Malty have lain back down to stay.
Alfie, Malty, what are we gonna do?
Sniffing and licking are all we ever do.

Walkies, walkies; let's walk for something to do.
Walking, walking around the lake with you.
Naughty, naughty! Play nice with the ducks and swans.
Naughty, naughty! You both have jumped into the ponds.
Alfie and Malty swimming around all wet, so happy and proud.
Alfie, Malty, now back home, dry, safe, and sound.

Back home now, barking at the garden gate,
Barking at sounds like the milkman often makes,
Or barking, barking at absolutely naught.
Alfie and Malty start to lick their snouts
Because licking and sniffing are what it's all about.
A dog's life to me, without a shadow of a doubt,
Looks like fun, licking one's snout!

Alfie and Malty start to roll around,
Just like wrestlers playing on the ground.
Snarling as they roll, they pretend to rock and roll.
Alfie and Malty sure have got some soul.

Alfie and Malty back at the garden gate,
Barking at the noises the street often makes.
Now you have seen what a dog's life is like,
Alfie and Malty will make you feel all right.

Oh no! Look out! The cat has come back too.
What do you think Alfie and Malty will do?
Yes, woofing and barking you know they really like,
Barking and howling throughout the long night.
If you do, too, you won't be the only one.
Have a go, kids; it looks like lots of fun!

Chasing the cat over the garden gate,
Oh, how a dog's life is just so great!
Alfie, Malty, you are my best mates.
But oh, no! Don't go over the garden gate.

My hands are full with these two clowns.
Never a day with any sort of frown.
They're going for a car ride and start jumping around.
They woof at the people passing by,
Woof at the sun and the bright blue sky,
Woof at the songs the radio plays.
Alfie and Malty have fun every day.

Alfie and Malty, what are we gonna do?
Once again life is so great with you.
Now it's time for tea; picky eaters they be—
No junk food; oh, maybe a treat or two,
A sneaky burger or bone for them from you.

Bellies full and tired from play,
Alfie and Malty lie and rest for the day.
See you soon! Dream of the next day's fun.
Morning comes soon, and then sleep is done.
Look out: Malty's dreaming of somewhere far.
I bet he's dreaming about woofing in the car.

Time to say goodbye to Alfie and Malty,
Who love to play and roll around,
Sniffing and licking their snouts.
You know that's what it's all about.
Dogs enjoy every moment of life, without a doubt.
Alfie and Malty, that is what we will do:
Enjoy life together, me and the both of you.

I hope you have enjoyed Alfie and Malty's things to do.
Try it sometime—sniff and play the whole day through.

BOOK II

Malty & Alfie & Teddy 2

Malty & Alfie & Teddy 2

Hi kids once again back to see your favorite pals malty alfie and guess who, yes a puppy named teddy chew
Teddy who? You'll see soon that's what teddy likes to do

A new puppy came this year to stay,
a puppy by the name of teddy, as soon as teddy came to stay we all knew almost straight away we should put our socks and shoes away, before teddy starts to chew them all away,

Chewing this and chewing that malty thought we'll get teddy to get that cat
Alfie didn't seem to keen Alfie thought teddy was a bit mean, especially when teddy started to chew the wire and plug to the washing machine

chewing this and chewing that teddy even chewed on uncle matt, nibbling toilet roll teddy would eat, he'd leave a pile of town paper near your feet, chewing this and chewing that even before we teached him to sat,

Morning till night teddy would chew, chew chew
The whole day through, oh no look he has got my shoes
chaseing his tale that's his new thing yes he is even chewing on that thing, round and round he
has to get bourd chewing his tale all day that can be assured,

Teddy chewing even a chair leg may be we'll get him a bone instead
For teddy to chew yes raw hide or a beef bone or two
That's the best thing to do
Now teddy is happy is happy with his new bone to chew

Hey teddy's going through a lot of bone have you noticed you, chewing and chewing held by
his paws, super ted we call him, but then we nicknamed him jaws
ohhhh chewing this and chewing that, we all feel for uncle matt, now teddy has learnt to jump,
chewing biting and now he can jump, oh how uncle matt is going to get the hump,

Teddy teddy we love you, you little terror stop eating me shoe
Teddy teddy chew chew chew, hope to see you all soon
Teddy teddy yes he has still got my shoe

The end

BOOK III

Orange Satsuma And Letters

Orange Satsuma and Letters

It's between 2002 and 2019, this story follows a young man and his family through some weird years turbulent years, dramatic events and quite frankly GHOSTLY Events or paranormal activity which takes place at their home.

Chapter One

Chris was in his early twenty's when he noticed strange events, going on at his home, it was a cloudy Sunday morning 3:30 am or even a Wednesday afternoon and a Sunday evening during a powercut, Chris witnessed several apparitions and strange events which lead him to an ongoing conclusion that a ghost was trying to contact him or provoke an reaction from him or his family or was it just his and his family's imagination running away with them,

Chris is a light hearted young man east going artistic, ambitious but knew his limitations from a young age, entertaining his family at every opportunity he could, he was into the usual social events, work was a bit non existing because of some bad luck with his health.

Living with his family Teena his mother also had health issues which made her a bit hard nosed and mental skitso with some real issues with abandonment, infidelity and missing possessions, all so Teena was sometimes annoyed by her neighbours, mostly her husband bob was all ways pulling some nerve it was not all bad Teena was a kind hearted angel hilarious, kirky, and helpful, Teena kind of looked a bit like dawn french with a big bottom,

Bob a seventy year old pensioner with bad knees a quiet man who attracted mayhem where ever he went along with friends he had white hair cute old scallywag, compo out of last of the summer wine would best describe him, some of the looks he would give you and the larking about on the market would have you in fits of larghter the pair of them together was a hoot, a time Chris can recall Teena was out in the garden on a rainy Tuesday afternoon painting the garden fence in the rain.

Then bob with one of his one liners like his excuses for dodging a bath he would say that a "bath might kill him due to the water being too high", or riggma "roll" "by eaek" in some old farm talk, he was a true gemwith white hair, he was like a puppy dog you could not stay mad at long, hard working with a fighting attitude and would never give up,

Chris's brother matt was a big brute of a man loves his grub loves beer and riding his 125cc chopper motorbike, matt worked with his dad, bob, on the market stall also with Teena selling tools and cleaning supplies, quite ironic really bob selling stuff like soap, shower gels and cleaning product but did not like to use them,

When Chris was young he and matt would be packed carefully in pillows and blanket duvets in the back of a red renault van on market days every Saturday and Sunday at 4am to 6am, we would have a great time on the markets hunting giant rats which would come out of the ditch's near the river, tip over hay stacks to catch volves and small mice, hunt around the markets buying burgers and bullets from the army stall, candy floss and party poppers.

Finding new friends to make trouble and mischief with, summers would fly by, wonder the auction rooms and stalls for hours, once we had formed a group of friends we would find some sort of play area usually a tractor pen or farm yard filled with exciting and dangerous toys like tractor wheels, one summer a boy from one of the stall holders area he had brought a pellet gun, we ended up along a field tipping hay stacks and trying in vain to shoot the wild life which ran off, we never hit anything but it kept us busy for hours.

Come and go when our childhoods summers came and went with the wind, Chris left the market life when he left school collage came calling and the sheer ideas of 3 am starts sent a shiver down Chris's back, matt continued with his dad to the present day adding hard wear to the cleaning, bath, and house products, the stall was doing all right

(picture) STALL MARKET AND TRAILER

all most like delboy and rodney in peckham anywhere they could put up the stall they would be a market places like cattle markets street corners car parks and sports halls, community centres money was being made the hard way Saturdays and Sundays without fail and two or three days in the week.

Chapter Two

It was a normal typical day bob, matt up earlie and out to work as normal Teena up with them to prepare lunch and flasks of tea, Chris in bed would often wake to the smell of food and coffee being poured, or at the sounds of cutlery, Chris awoke on this morning it was a cold mid-winter morning Chris brushe's the sleep from his eyes and heads to the bathroom to take care of that business and swill his hands and face.

Chris walks tiredly into the front bedroom his parents slept in, walks around the double bed to look out the window to see if bob and matt had left up the street in their van as he often did, but this time as Chris walked towards the window the curtin was being held up by the corners like something was already at the window looking out, the curtin droped back and flopped back to its static position as Chris stopped and looked straight at the window open mouthed, what had Chris just seen,it was like a dream Chris thought to himself, was he still dreaming or was he going mad, he stood thinking for a moment wondering what to say or do with what he had just seen.

Chris gathers himself and heads down stairs where bob matt, and Teena are still in the kitchen preparing to leave for work, it's still dark outside pitch black with a whispery light cold wind the back door is fully open in anticipating the departure of the two workers all the lights were on, Chris stands in the door way and begins to try to not look insane or weird and tell them about the event upstairs "bob", "don't be silly Chris you're in a fantasy world "bob laughed out, Teena at first looks as if she believes what Chris just said about the curtin but shrugs her shoulders and says " it's the wind Chris",

Chris looks at mum and says: "oh yer", he begins to prepare some eggs on the stove as matt and bob head off to work and Teena to heads back upstairs, as Chris flips the eggs on to the toast in the empty kitchen Chris senses the wind on his back like his brother had walked into the kitchen door forgetting his coat, Chris turned to greet matt and no one was there the door closed shut and quiet as space.

Again Chris's face dropped to the floor in fear, his heart thumping like a base drum, its all he can hear, the eerie silence and empty kitchen stood still his eggs getting cold he grabs the plate and coffee quickly wipes the kitchen clean and hurriedly hops it upstairs to get dressed, What a start to the day that was.

Later on that day, late afternoon Teena and Chris were having afternoon tea and chocolate digestives talking about things and about what Chris had seen, Chris "do you belive me mum,what I saw this morning ", Teena ":yes I believe you Chris but as I said it was probably the wind or your imagination or something, "" it's hard to prove anything when it's that sort of thing, "you need video or sound recordings or something, ", you know",

Chris": yes, but look at what I saw," I am sure it was not the wind the curtin was being held up as if someone was holding it in the air if i had recorded it i am sure that there is a ghost or apparition here with us"

Teena :" arrgh yes no, maybe, yes let's just get on and see what happens ",Chris:"i know it is hard to believe," I wouldn't believe me either ":"it's confusing, misleading, and scary to open up and realise the unknown, it can be difficult"

Chris:"just remember your past Teena you were always saying a long time ago you can hear voices at he kitchen sink when washing up", and those dreams you had in your past where you said you were being held down in your bed with a man holding you down, the night screams matt had where he was being squished by a vise in the small spare bedroom, the room where it is always too hot or far too cold, " he used to wake up in cold hot sweats"

The pair sit and sip their tea and coffee at the kitchen table and ponder about the situation for a few moments until they both get bored and Teena notices that her tv program has just started.

A few days go by before the next incident it's a Wednesday afternoon in winter, it is raining heavy outside, raining most of the day dark clouds not very pleasant to be outside, bob and matt come home earlier from working on the stall market, all the family stand talking and making tea and cheese sandwiches, matt and bob talking about the day's events, bob:"says :"whoo you should have seen the rain this morning it was bucketing down the street partially flooded the water nearly took some of the stock down the street,"the day was a complete wash out until the people come out and wanted umbrellas for some reason,"

Chris giggles and goes towards the cupboard to get the tomatoe ketchup to put on his cheese toast, he opens the cupboard door slowly as normal the cupboard where the tinned food is kept, he then jumps back and flinches at the sight of a tin of orange satsumas segments flying out the shelve towards the floor,Chris": "did you just see that guys the tin nearly hit me, it flew out of the cupboard at me",

bob:" really nargh, no way boy,"

Teena :"arrgh you pulling our legs, you're joking"

matt:"no way its the cupboard fault or something the tin must have been packed up against the door or something,"

Teena :" yer thats it,"

Chris:"no way i have just cleaned the shelves this morning I tidied the shelve and put the tins what were in the cupboard all in a line and nothing stacked up high because of the amount of tins that were in there, " only three or four tins were in the storage cupboard being midweek and shopping was done on Saturday the cupboard was normally bear,

Chris:"yes matt again that would be the answer matt but there wasn't any canns stacked up, "that would happen if the tinns were stacked up two or three high, " NOW matt EXPLAIN that detective columbo

Matt:" ohh oooh, arrgghh, yes, give a dog a bone sir,",:" it must be," matt stuttered for a moment thinking of a new reason for the tin of flying fruit,

The family talk for hours about different reasons for the active tin of satsumas, bob even has a look on his face like wide eyed and a bit shook at the ideas, they all shake they heads in confused acceptation of what is going on, bob turns to his account books and matt goes for a lie down and Chris goes and potters about a bit all go and get on with their busy life's for the rest of the rainy day.

All seem to forget to get on with the day to day tasks, that's all you can ever do I suppose, just get on and hope the answer reveals itself, but I suppose it's in the back of each person's mind, if they believe what has happened, the events of ghostly apparition's preys on each of them individually not knowing if what is happening is the supernatural or just usual day to day stuff, voices and door scrapping's can be explained.

Month's would fly by as they seem to do with no incident or apparition presenting itself to the family effecting the family's mood, then a cluster of events that seem to throw Chris's way of thinking there would be days or mornings where Chris would wake up to what sounded like our neighbours shouting voodoo noises or weird language like talking in toungs, pure gibberish, it was a 5:30am start and on a spring morning, only what can be described as quiet shouting Teena would be half asleep and often ill, but she would respond to the weird shouting as if it was aimed directly at her,Chris jumped up out of bed whilst this shouting quiet was going on looking out the window,Teena 's in the back garden and a unknown man was standing directly behind our back fence the image was blurry but it was a man, our house was adjacent to the railway and a old peoples home was direct out the back gate at the end of the garden, the image of the man in the morning light made identifying him hard but Chris could hear him and Teena and bob talking, the unknown man was standing seeming to talk loudly to himself but with Teena and bob talking over the top of them both somewhat like to interrupt or effect their conversation, quite rude really but also strange at that time of morning, it only lasted a few moments this back and forth between mum and dad saying bye to each other and this weird person interrupting with weirdly use of the English language, almost like Teena would be saying:" ok bob see you later:, and bob says:"ok can you do that thing in the dryer for me:" and over the top at the same time the strange man would say:"SEE ME THEN SEE YOU:" you then HAVE TO DO:", NO" copercative seperative slample " slvaving tramming to slightlystif inn:" kind of over the top immersing into the conversation, weird

The man then slipped off back into the old peoples home and never seen again, Chris, thinking to himself, if I say anything about this I am going to look mad myself, because when confronting Teena and bob later on that same day both had no recollection there was some one there at all talking over them,

Voices in the house at night would increase only at night time Chris regularly found himself being woke up at 1 am or 3am with screams and tapping on the stair case landing outside his room, one evening it sounded like little feet were walking about the loft space.

Moving of possessions about the home was a common occurrence one afternoon the curtins in the front drawing room were blinds which needed cleaning, Chris decided to go ahead and clean the blinds, even if the procedure is quite demanding, the counter weight's at the bottom of the blinds need to slide out from each individual blind and each blind sheet taken down socked and clean dried then put back making sure that the weight and chain lines up with each other, if not the chain would not aline and the curtins would never close, Chris had done this two three times or more at home and thinking nothingof the hardness of the cleaning procedure Chris just got stuck in,

Before long the job was done, being a sunny spring day the sunshine heat helped with the drying of each blind on the washing line, the job flew by taking just two hours to complete from start to finish, Chris had tea in the same room as the blinds checking looking up at the new brightness of the bleached blinds and the hot spring evening light sunshine cascading through the blinds, Wonderful,

Thing is Chris came down stairs the following morning and the blinds were facing the wrong way all the counter balance weights were around the opposite way he left them and pulling the blind cord would not open the blinds correctly as he knew that he had done the blinds correct because he sat and looked out the window at the street and sunshine eating his tea the previous evening, Chris had to then take each weight out and turn it around to face the room, this made Chris quite made and confronted the members in the house hold as you would, you would not think it was a ghost straight away you would believe it was your dad or mum, brother playing a massive prank on you, but no, none of the family came forward.

After the confrontation Chris asking the family had they messed with the curtins, Chris realised that neither of them can pull that off, mum was disabled with her legs and dad with his bad knees and matt was a sleep all morning having work and other troubles on his mind.

Chris decides to move forward a few months go by, Chris wakes up, a brand new day, lovely morning meets Chris in June,the family getting on with life as normal, Chris gets up and packs his swimming sports bag for his weekly physio session at the local swimming pool he visits once twice weekly because of doctors advise to help with a bad back and some arthritic conditions Chris has from a bad accident he had as a child involving a bike and a car.

Chris would swim for one or two hours gets out showers the usual routine, this day he walked in to town for some light shopping home by late afternoon packs his bag out on to the work surfaces, prepares a well-deserved meal, after the meal heads up stairs for a nap walking and swimming takes it out of Chris, later on bob matt, and Teena are all home preparing the evening meal just after six pm, Teena prepares the food with the shopping bob, matt brought home from the market,, Chris awakes from his quick nap and comes down stairs in his tee shirt and track suit bottoms, settling down to watch the evenings television, peace and harmony fill the air on the warm summer night, until around nine ten pm Chris hears some scrapping and thumping noises, he turns his head from the tv to position his ears up stairs, the noise seems to be coming from upstairs from Chris's room

Chris gets up with a groan and wonders up the stairs to the middle step to hear what is going on in his room, the noise sounds to Chris like people moving the bed or running up and down the room he walks up the stairs because the noise seems to not be stopping he opens the door and walks into his room, NOTHING, no sign of any body in the room he looks around turns on the light but nothing

Chris :" shouts down stairs to his mum, Chris "mum did you hear that noise, Teena :"no, what is it, Chris:"I don't know there is a thumping noise in my room or scrapping noises can you hear anything from down there, Teena :" no nothing at all, I can't hear anything,

Chris moves over to the window and looks out the window opening the curtin's Chris suddenly notices an imprint on the window, on the outside of the paine of glass what can be only described as talken powder mark, image or chalk dust or even moth wing dust, almost like finger pring dust a fine image of a small bald headed troll like image print of a man with large big protruding eye sockets with a small body, arms open wide showing ribs and the outline of a very small man in white powder, Chris at this point thinking it was an alien, the dust image was no bigger than a five pound note two, three inches radius in the middle of the window,

Chris gets matt and shows him the image straight away Chris asks him to take a picture on his swanky new mobile phone but it would not take the picture because of no memory space Chris:" oh I do not believe this when you need a picture the phone camera won't work typical,"

matt:" yep it won't allow me to take the image, any way it looks like a pig den or starling bird try' d to fly in through the window or something", "I'm off" matt says wanting to get back to his tv shows, Chris is left standing by the window frustrated with technology and grabs a pencil and draws the image for future reference,

The following morning Chris try 's again with another camera but he image will not come through due to the lighting issue you would have needed a much better camera, leaving the image a few days it's still there, he wonders if to get the news or a professional camera person but like reality it often bites hard, when there is work and other testing things going on Chris just forgets and try to think ahead moving on.

Late June arrives as soon as it comes it is soon gone again, Chris decides to fill his evening with some June gardening whilst the light is good and its warm outside, he decides to clean up some potted plant pots and tidy the seating area of summer dust, Chris sweeps and sorts the garden area just directly outside the kitchen back door as he sits and digs the soil Teena and bob, both standing in and around the kitchen bob notices something quite strange going on

Bob:" look Teena come here take a look out the window at Chris in the garden",

Teena :" oh bob what is it, what is Chris doing now, "

bob:", no," just come and look, its looks amazing really look quick",

Teena ambles across to the window and Teena and bob stare quite bemused at Chris in the garden outside, what they are seeing is Chris sitting on the, garden bench potting about with his twowl mud with what seems to be ten to twenty five white glowing lights floating around his head like a swarm of moths or fire flies it was late evening just around eight o'clock, bob rubs his eyes in amazement, Chris seems to notice them as well but he seems to think they are just the dust or flies that normally surround your head in summer but from Teena s and bob's view from the window the sight was just magical the white orbs floating and as if anticipating Chris's hand movements the white orbs seem to dance around Chris's head reating to his movements like a cosmic nature dance this went on for a good couple of minutes dancing and floating around his head, as bob slowly walks out side to see better the orbs just seemed to disappear like snow or fly to somewhere out of sight melt away like snow,

Bob:" hey Chris did you just see that over your head so, "there was lights, orbs floating around your head"

Chris:" eerrr yer i saw it it was dust or somthing dam flys"

Bob:" yyeeaarrrr, :," no Chris ", "we saw lights floating around your head", "like snow dancing around with your movements"

Chris:" Really ", "WOW " well you know i did notice them but as you know you don't know these days what is up or down do you, something weird one day is normal the next "quite hard to tell what is real or false these days"

Bob:" yes son, yes I know what you mean, "that was a bit strange"

The summer went with a bang here one minuet and November before you can catch your breath, months would fly by with ease work, life and other family events come and go with ease, work routine and family matters, the family would often talk about the events of ghostly goings on,

Christmas was a good one that year but for all the electric problems they had a week before Christmas the washing machine blew out the belt or motor problems, then the usual Christmas lights blew on the Christmas tree and in the window, then the hover started as normal as Chris plugged it in but before he started to hover the wire started to catch fire and smoke, the family gather in the front room with the smell of smoke in the air and look at each other with smirky worrie on their face, matt says :" what is going on are we in that movie gremmlins or something, "

Teena :replies:" i hope the gremlins go away soon we can't cope much longer with this :"

Chris smiles and agrees with matt and Teena :" Chris:" my bank balance is screaming at me fist the hover then the lights and washing machine, it must be a curse or something, matt have you strood on any black cats or rabbits or something,"

As if by Chris's words of worries a popping noise came from the kitchen, and bob's screams, bob:"arrrggghhhhh quick Teena, "come in hear quick" they enter the kitchen and se the oven off and looking black from the in side

bob: "it just went pop, I ain't done ought," the kitchen oven had seemed to overheat and pop, broken on December 24th what could go wrong next as Christmas day came it was not ruined at all because Chris was a real good cook he seemed not fazed and cooked the meal by gass hob only even the Yorkshire pudding all cooked in a frying pan.

It was a cold January out shopping in the sales to buy a new hover and cooker Chris awoke early to get a good start on the cold day it was quite early in the morning, dark still outside Chris walks down stairs to get coffee and toast slowly ambles up the stairs and sits on the bed rubbing the sleep out of his eyes and toast crumbs into his eyes.

Sipping his coffee and gazing out of the window at the morning sky and condensation on the window facing east watching as the morning sun rose very slowly, now around six am the quiet spoiled by a loud thud coming from the bathroom next to Chris's room a thud noise like a person had just fell over or slumped to their knees, Chris looks up and fear comes across Chris's face his heart starts to beat fast and pound in his ears the sound of nothing seeming to get even louder than noise,

A kind of hissing in Chris's ears, the sound of silence yhis was the scariest he had become in a long while with what has been going on recently who wouldn't be a little scared at thudding noises, Chris does not know what to do at first, the fear consuming his whole body the second thing to cross Chris's mind is that is it a burglar outside his room

Chris moves slow standing up tip toes to the bedroom door and quietly listens to the other side he stands at the door in a fear haze like every second took an hour to pass, he slowly opens the door and peers into the hall and bathroom just left of his room, and sees nothing, he gains confidence and opens the door fully and speeds up his movements and moves quickly to avoid the squeaky floor boards and heads to the cover of the stair case and peers down stair's from the top of the banister he sees what he thinks is the outline of a man in black standing and slowly trying to walk up stairs the shadowy figure a dark smoky image,Chris does not flinch when he sees the dark formation, fear has now took over his entire body as Chris takes a deep breath and blinks putting his hand over his mouth like you do, trying to hold his fear and emotions inside, one side of him wants to run and hide and the other wants to say hello to the dark figure coming upstairs, as his eyes open the image has gone like as fast as it came it went,

Chris stands up and looks down at the place the dark shadow figure was, and slumps to his knees, quite exhausting this was becoming, he runs into his parents room to tell them what he had just seen, both Teena and bob were fast asleep Chris wakes them to tell them both, Chris:" you know what I've just seen,"

Teena :"what the boogy electritial maniac again " Chris:" yep, ! Well " yes something like that " on the bottom of the stairs a man stood like in all black or something,"

Teena and bob looked shocked,bob:" really Chris another ghost aren't we getting to be so popular", " I mean quite a lot of activity going on around here " !,

Chris:" yes i know, it wasn't you in the bathroom a little while ago was it, bob :" "noi have just woken up, Teena :" no same here i have just got up as you came in ", Chris:" I just heard someone fall over it was very loud i was really bricking myself real scared like, ", they continue to talk, bob sees the time and says "why" so early " can't you tell our ghost to call later on",

Chris goes to the stair landing to see if any clues had been left, Teena and bob set the snooze button for eight o clock, Chris hunts the stair way and turns the light on but there was nothing to be found, what had he heard what had he seen maybe in time it will be made clear, the morning seemed to drag on and on after that start, Chris looks out of the front window and sees only the milk man and a speedy fox running up the street, he becomes all emotional thinking what could be up with the events going's on was it dead family trying to contact them, or did the house they live in have a nasty past,

The morning continues, as eight thirty comes and shopping January sales awaits the family, matt's friend James comes' around as normal shouts at the gate to get his attention a few beers and good times, the kitchen is full of bags and paper rapping new hover and shopping bags the family talk and munch on goodies brought from the shopping centre mall,

late evening the family prepared meals and television what more do you need, matt and James get beers flowing chilling out its like the morning event had never took place, Chris cooks spag bolognaise and sits cozy in his favorite seat, the evening usual tv shows Teena bob off to bed around ten thirty the game of footie comes on and the bellies start to rumble again after a few beers, we all grab the take out menu to get a take away before the footie highlights come on and pass out on the couch with late night football,

This was what usually went on Saturday into Sunday if they weren't working that is, Sunday morning usual again not much going on Sunday roast songs of praise and washing machine working overtime, This Sunday night was a close night very cold and clear outside clear starry sky and when i say cold it was almost freezing, crisp and quiet, it was a round midnight but seemed a lot earlier the NFL was on,

Teena sitting snoozing at the tele and Chris in the living room, Chris gets up and checks the back garden just for something to do, stretching his legs, when entering the back door again a pop and complete darkness ensues the whole house, a power cut hits the whole area streets wide, Chris:" just as the NFL getts going to the best bit," great A POWER CUT" "great" "aaarrrggghh " COME ON "

, Teena :" oohhh i told you to change the channel i can't stand American football"

Teena get's up and goes to sit with sleeping bob on the couch, Chris goes to hunt for some candles

, Teena :" wait Chris it's a power cut it will be back on soon, "

PICTURE PHONE HALLWAY BLUE WINDOW IMAGE

Chris hunts for candles and a tourch, he grabs what he can and walks down stairs the power cut normally would come on straight away but as it was a Sunday evening this power cut was a long one, Chris had time to walk up the street and standing at the top of the street looking as far as he could see the streets were as black as space and so quiet, you would never see this too many times in your life, streets as dark as if a terrorist had blew the power station or streets like old London town in 1655, or a movie shoot where the star would stand in the fore ground and the street lights would all come on towards the star, it was a beautiful sight, Chris takes it all in the winter glow was amazing, The moon big and bright in the sky, frost glittering in the moon light lighting up the dark street as if it was a summers day,

Chris walks back inside takes his winter coat off and places it in the usual place, as Chris places his coat on the banister near the phone by the stairs he glances at a blue shimmering moon lit man walking down the ally, Chris thinks matt is home or the neighbours are outside but when nothing comes in,matt nowhere to be seen, Chris goes out to investigate what is in the ally, Chris notices his neighbours car not there and matt was still out, neighbours gate locked from the inside,

Chris steps into the kitchen and tells mum and dad about what he had just seen Chris:" am i going mad " I keep seeing weird things and it's becoming a regular event," Teena :" yes never mind love " bob:" har har Chris don't worry Your little bonce"

Chris :" don't worry I would love to stop worrying but or house guest's keep making it hard, i think we should open a guest house for the living dead, maybe call it guest house paranormal or something along those lines,

The lights in the street and home finally pop on as they continued to talk about things and finally the family get to bed after the usa American football show around 3 am,

The winter took its toll that year on the family home,a small drip in the extension roof after some heavy snow in February the water would slowly form a drip of water, then loudly fall into a bucket, after a while the roof hole got bigger and a crack opened up with black mould.

Chris would say to his dad when are we going to get the roof leak fixed, bob would reply as would Teena, we need money for the van, to keep the market going Chris, the family had insurance but the insurance company would not pay for the roof due to some regulation of policy cause and effect or something along those lines saying how the roof got in that state and they would not cover it, same old story with insurance companies

The drip continued through the year Chris would worry every time he looked at the hole which now looked like a round dark saucer with black patterns all around the dripping hole, it kind of looked like a smiling face with eyes looking down with a cheeky smile grinning down, the black mould kind of dried up around the drip stopping the drip from time to time

, the family came over for dinner grandmother,auntie, and nephews, Chris would point it out to all in the family trying to gain support for the ghostly events, Chris pointed up to the mould stain and says Chris:"looook at that all most through how is the water being stopped :" dad we need to get that sorted ", Chris's grandmother: "would say :"oohh yes that needs sorting,,"i wish i could help you guys but i can't afford my own house repair let alone your problems",

Raising the subject of the roof Chris's grandmother would talk for ages with the family, Joan had just lost her husband Chris's grandfather some years back to liver cancer Joan would say"

I as well have been experiencing some ghostly events, my husband comes and visits me in my dreams" I have had some dreams of moving stuff, cloths being moved and weird noise's at night time"

Chris:" yes nan you would not believe the things going on here, we have had noises and moving of all sorts", " I now believe that ghost's do visit us somehow, we just need some good evidence to prove the fact that ghostly apparitions are among us, the living,"

Joan :" yes i think there has to be some sort of energy transference or memories somewhere down the line, with all the emotions of going through the death process, we must be able to have some impact on each other in the next life"

Chris:" if only we could get some video or sound evidence we can show people that the paranormal is out there and active here,"

Joan :" but what would you do with the evidence and who do you show the evidence to, will the evidence truly make whom you show it to believe the evidence you show, "well you will have to wait for an opportunity and see

Chris on this day sees his nan and auntie out, kissed' both on the cheek, Chris: "see you soon nan, mum has got your shopping order of cleaning supplies you can pop over later to pick them up,

Joan :"yes thanks Chris I will pop over later to pick them up when mum and dad are back,"see you later",

Chris often thought about his grandfather he was close too when he was a younger boy, Chris would often also dream about his granddad Chris would be at his granddad's house in the back garden playing by the apple tree and climbing to grab some apples all the family would be there parties in the garden bbq, weekends.

The dreams would be vivid and real, in one of the vivid dreams Chris and matt was dropped off by they granddad in the car his grandad had at the time a grey large rover, Chris would walk in the door and his grandad would shout bye as they drove past,Chris would awake hearing his grandads voice in the bed room and stair way, opening his eyes's blurry vision Chris would shout out thinking his grandfather was there with him, Chris jumped up out of his bed to see if it was real, but it wasn't all it was a cozy loverly dream about his wonderful grand father

since the death of his grandfather Chris had often seen his grandfather or thought he did any way someone who would look similar to him walk like him or drees the same way Chris would see him every day, behind him at the supermarket, or at the swimming pool his grandfather was all ways with him where ever he went,

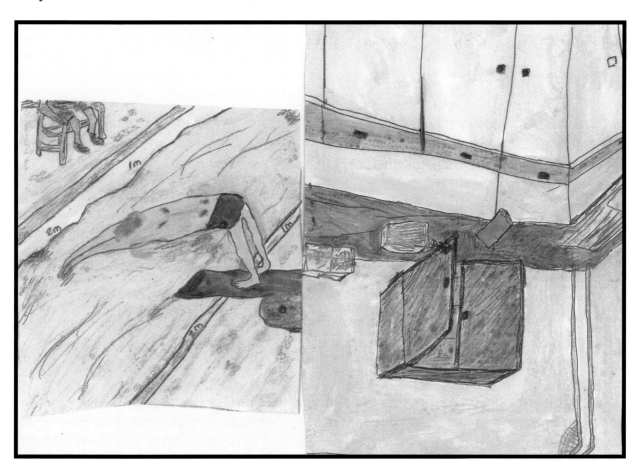

8o clock that evening on a Friday Joan came back around to pick her shopping Teena had left out for her Joan :"hey guys how are you all only me," look i have brought you this cake i baked this week, " your favorite chocolate and double chocolate, "

Teena :" oohhh mother you should have you know i can just eat a slice or three of that, i can tell you," great"

bob :" arrrggh good thanks Joan you said you made it your self did you"

Joan :" yes Julia helped me"

Auntie Julia:" yes i gave a hand i mixed the chocolate icing and cracked the eggs", "don't you just love choccy cake,"

All the family gather around the cake, tea and coffee pot starts to rattle and the family sit and relax and start to natter about the days events

bob:" aaarrrggghhh, " this is nice put the tv on Teena," " Joan did you see the news about the budget the government are doing just as much as they did a year ago, nought, ", "labour party doing well,"

Joan :" yes i saw the news same old same old stuff, seen it all before, " a little more money for elderly and the poor, "

matt: "yer the budget dad, nan, everyone i have a joke, "THE GOVERNMENT"

all start laughing, matt: "No wait that isn't the joke ",

they burst out laughing any way, as they stop laughing matt tells his joke he heard on the market this week, Matt:" If mothers have mother's day and fathers have father's day, what do single blokes have, matt pause's waits for the family to say something, then says the ending, ;" Teena :" arrghh I think i have heard this one"

Julia:" yes I think I have as well"

Matt:" THEY HAVE PALM SUNDAY", Chris, Teena, bob Joan and Julia all laugh chuckling along in a little descust but enjoying the joke,

Chris says:" I have one for you, a woman walks into a doctors surgery complaining about that she has got some strawberries stuck up inside her, the doctor says don't worry love, I have got some cream for that,"

they all start laughing, and continue to chat along with coffee, tea and cake, Chris goes into the other room to watch and record some recordings on his phone, he closes the door to record the theme tune of a movie sound track on to his phone for a ring tone, makes sure no sounds from the kitchen interferes with the recording, stores the recording and sett's his phone down for later,

The night draws to an end the family says they good byes for the night

some years fly by with nothing happening, new neighbours move into the street and Chris's I T course's and work with charity organisations leave Chris with little or no time, looking after the home and saving money for the roof took all the family's strength, they dealt with everything like every family do to get by, but struggling through life the hard way,

bob had some bad luck just before the Christmas gathering, literally the 23rd of December the van they use for the markets decided to go wrong the suspension totally gave way costing a whopping nine hundred pounds straight away and had to be paid in full, which was the total savings of the year to pay for Christmas and the roof fund,

as the year went the roof got worse and every rainy day became a dash in the morning to replace the bucket of rain water, things were on the edge for quite some time scrapping bye day to day Teena 's health became worse leaving Chris and matt to take on more with the day to day running of the house,

the family get together on morning to discuss the the phone bill, to discuss the price of the bill and also to find out who was using the phone calling the exotic places, they argue at first blaming each other for the phone bill, then after a lengthy discussion all the family decided to not use the phone or record each time they used the home phone in the hall by the window, each would write time and number and length of call on a booklet by the home phone

When three months past the anticipation of the 3 month, quarterly phone bill by post was intense each member waiting who would get it in the neck from dad,

the morning of the phone bill came bob and Teena sat down at the kitchen table and put the kettle on reading through the bill pages and cross referencing the booklet with the phone bill which gave time number and call length on three or four page's, bob and Teena start to read and become puzzled

Chris: "what is it what dose the phone bill say"

Teena :" well the bill isn't too high " : "but they is something strange going on " the bill seems to read wrong, it says the phone is being used late at night or when we are out"

bob", yer, I get that as well"

Chris looks over the page's as well and they are right the days where the family are all out either at work or sleeping the phone seems to be being used, and phone numbers with area codes in Florida, or southern America, south African number's, places like domincom republic the family look at each other in bemused confusement each wondering what is going on, Teena totally loses the plot thinking it is a neighbour or the woman next door, Chris points out to matt,bob and Teena to ring the numbers to see who they are, bob:" yes good idear"

Chris grabs the phone number to one of the numbers that don't add up where it shows the family was definitely out of the hoes to use a land line home phone,, Chris dials the long number and waits for a response when the phone answers Chris listens to the woman on the end of the line, in a foreign accent she says, " hello delmonte head office how can i help you please",

Chris:" delmonte " what the HELL "

lady on phone:" excusesome, sir, thankenyou which is it you require sir please,"

Chris replies" you are delmonte head office"

lady on phone :" YEEss sir how may i beings of helpings to you sir"

Chris:"well i have a problem my phone bill says we keep phoning you on this number,"

lady on phone:" yeeessss sir i seeing your problem sir, you needing to buying's some produce,"

Chris:" uuurrrrrgggghhh, no my phone bill says we keep ringing you but we have not rang you at all

lady on phone:" aaarrrrgggghhhhh yes now i seeing, i will put you through to billing sir, please waitings a moment"

Chris, :" NO wait"

Chris puts the phone down because the cost was going to be high, and goes to sit in the kitchen with mum and dad, Chris :" well its delmonte

bob:" delmonte", " isn't that the tinned fruit company"

Chris:" yes that is the tinned fruit company"

Teena :" delmonte :" you must be out of your mind,

after that the phone got cut off, bob was not having that,

all the family agreed to the cutting off of the phone all of them got pay as you go phones in stead and try'd to move forward with their life, saving and scrapping to save for the pending desastor of the extention roof, would it hold another year, or would the rain gush through and destroy the kitchen, life trundled by day after day

the new neighbours next door was a bit of a struggle it seemed that each year they stayed the new neighbours got worse year to year, it started out a small four person family then they had baby after baby and by the time they moved out they was seven of them, loud screaming would start from 9 o clock am to 9 o clock pm daily through the summer with a daily bbq in the garden which the family cooked nan bread on,

Then they chopped down the long standing trees on their property which made the sound worse, it sort of echoed up into the house from the garden, the bin situation kind of exploded one summer the new neighbours bin was kept in the ally way, much to the annoyance to Chris and bob because the ally was not the place for a large bin due to the small narrow exit and entrance every time you would come home you would smell a dirty bin filled with hot wet nappies and food bin bags, well it exploded all right the bin was over filled and the flys, big black and green, blue black flies spent the day there in the bin in the ally, Chris was watching tv one evening when he went to get a breath of fresh air around 8 o clock and saw that some yellowy white things were climbing the wall at the back of the home, yes you might of guessed by now it was a swam of crawling maggots which had started life in the bin in the ally, they were crawling up in the air vents up the wall some got as high as six or seven foot high,

you could say life was not pleasant at all dealing with no work, and mothers bad health a leaking extension roof and an over friendly ghost which would scare the living out of Chris from time to time.

Some good times too a birthday party for matt, it was a Saturday bob and Teena got home and prepared food and party stuff for matt, matt was in the bath getting ready for the night out with friends, the plans were to have a afternoon early evening get together with family nan auntie mum and dad then a good night painting the town red with vodka and gin mixers,

grandmother came around with presents and more cake she loved to bake our nan, auntie rose come over with a present and cards, auntie Julia as well all family nephews and uncle's in the kitchen and home that year matt and Chris's friend James had to move in with his two dogs because of some girlfriend issues well i call it some marital problems but James call's it he's having b***h problems,

the family sat and celebrate matt's birthday Chris's nephews were usual quiet kids face's stuck in their phones Auntie Rose:" look at the kids Joan, look all ways into the phone where ever we go.

Chris hearing his auntie rose about the kids on the phone Chris:" argh i have a joke about phones i made it up the other day," pattene'd it and everything"," ready Guys" :" a bloke went into the pub and started to talk to his friend, he say's " i just found out what blue tooth is, his friend says yes have you, its a free message sending on phone or computer,, " yes that's it the bloke says but the thing is my dentist has been charging me for a blue tooth treatment plan when go to the dentist chair, "ooooohhhh, you have to watch out for that he is taking advantage of you," his friend say's", " yes my new dentist said the same thing to me this morning you have to keep on your guard at all times, " yer my new dentist has put me right now, he has moved me to a better plan now, the new plan is a lot cheaper, " it's the new blue ray treatment plan,he says that it is much better for my teeth, the family burst out screams of laughter fill the family's kitchen, the night flows as normal Chris, matt James go out on the town after the family leaves and a normal night out insues drinking and dancing Chris sits down after a go on the karaoke, Chris remembers that he wanted to change the ring tone on his phone but never got around to it Chris flicks his phone on and access's the phone tone menu and selects the recordings file, and selects a new tone, he put's the phone to his ear and listens out to his new recording and taken aback at what he hears the recording he had made and forgot about some time ago has got some kind of extra voice at the end of the recording, Chris decides to listen again and once again hears a mans voice saying something, Chris shows matt the evidence on his phone, he shows James as well, both say" no" you must of done that Chris it's you

the next day at home Chris comes down stairs, dad and mum are having brunch with some cake from the night before Chris pull's out the phone recording and shows mum and dad the recording both seem shocked and bemused at what they hear,

Bob:" well it is definitely a mans voice at the end saying something muffled

Teena :"it sounds like" up in there" or something", you can just make it out listen again,"

Chris plays the recording over and over and it seems to be a mans voice muffled voice "upings there", Chris tells all he see's what he had captured on his phone, older sister, even Chris's doctor got a listen to the recording, but as his grand mother said some time ago not many belived what they was hearing

months flew by again with no events Chris one day decides to go and see his grandmother to talk as they often did, Chris helped fix the kettle and clean the garden mess went to the shops to buy a new water tap which was leaking in his nans kitchen and talked about the problems of their week, Julia came in with the new developed photo pictures Joan had developed

Joan :"argh Chris take a look at the photos there are loads, there are some of the party and my holiday and some of granddad some time ago, Julia hands the photo's to Chris,and Chris flick's through each photo talking as he went about every photo with his nan, when he come's across some strange photos of grandad, the photo is of his grand father standing in Chris's kitchen in the 1970's with a small bag of satsumas in one hand and Chris as a one year old in the other arm

Chris shakes his head in amazement not at the dodgy shirt and jumper combination grand dad was wearing but at sight of grandad holding a bag of satsumas oranges

Chris :" look at this nan, it's grandad with me and some satsumas" "can you remember that ghost event some time ago a tin of fruit came out flying at me in my kitchen, can you remember can you",

Joan, :" yes i can Chris yes, " arrrrr it is grandad trying to contact you Chris ",i would not be surprised if he was trying to contact you he loved you so much, " both Joan and Chris sat and remembered grandad for a moment drinking tea and looking at more pictures, when silence came over the room not a sound they heard, until a tapping noise coming from Joan s loft,

Joan :" you hear Chris

Chris:" yeerrr

the sound was just like the sound of little feet running across the loft space, the lights twitched on and off in the living room and another banging tapping noise came from the kitchen,

Chris:" nan what is going on what do we do ",

Joan :"well Chris i guess just go with it enjoy and remember the good times and we will see grandad real soon,

<<missing image>>

Chris all emotional rode his bike home for dinner, the following day Chris lies on his bed remembering the photos and events of the day before, he decides to keep busy and clear his head by doing some cleaning he decides to go up in the roof loft space removes the square hatch and climbs up in the loft, the loft has bags and boxes placed near the hatch for easy grabbing, Chris climbs over the bags and boxes clearing and sorting as he goes, dust flying about the place Chris sorts the mess to a good standard and notices a set of cupboards or draws he sits next to the draws and looks in side, why has this draw set not been seen before was a thought Chris had, the bags and boxes looked to obscure the draw's existence Chris riffles through the draws and finds a bright blue sky blue box with jars and old tins from the 1980's and even tins from the 1950's, it looks like they were used to store stuff some are full with nails and rubber ends then opens this heavy feeling tin, he opens it with a ghasp the tin is filled with old pure gold coins, he places the tin to open more jars and old tins, one contained pure gold ring's and chains, diamonds the size of maltesers red rubies and yet more gold coins

Chris sits by the gold strune all over the floor, kneels to his knees in exhausting release their worries were over Chris thought to himself, fix the roof and sort out the house, Chris sits with his head in his hands thinking of his grandad knowing that he is still here with him and the family a smile comes across Chris's face knowing that he and granddad will meet again soon

What a predicament what a story

Is it real or is it fake

ooohhh for goodness sake

ghosts over here ghost's over there

please refrain from throwing fruit in my hair

so i can sleep with out a care

hopefully with clean dry underwear

by Christopher Terence knight 01/01/2019

POEMS

Untitled 1

This is how I'm feeling right now:
A mess I can't clean up. How I frown!
My world's been turned upside down.
Losing my dad left me quite numb.
Now I have gone and lost my mum.

Up in heaven now they rest,
putting my nerves to the test.
So I face the future with a smile and grin.
Please don't blame me
when I show up with the gin.

Can't be sad for too long; have to sing a different song
to all my friends who knew thee.
Facebook's where I'll be, find friends, and keep in touch.
Oh, thank you all so very much.

Got to wrap it up; it's time to go,
last orders and time at the bar.
Never mind, it's not too far.
The next life should be better than this.
I bid you all farewell with a great big kiss
from your friend, big, friendly Chris.
Come on, give us a big hug.
See you all down at the pub!

Untitled 2

What a predicament! What a story!
Is it real, or is it fake?
Oh, for goodness sake!
Ghosts over here, ghosts over there.
Please refrain from throwing fruit in my hair,
so I can sleep without a care—
hopefully with clean, dry underwear.
(1 January 2019)

Ko's ta Coffee: Coffee Shop Mate

Smell of coffee in the air,
here at the coffee shop, the price you must share.
Smell of coffee in the room,
coffee and cake; belly goes boom.

Sweet coffee down my throat.
Oops, where have I left my coat?
Another cup, that'll be great!
How I love coffee; another coffee, mate!

Smell of coffee in the air,
nothing else can compare.
A buzz to wake you from your sleep;
too many and then you can't sleep.
And you may leave the shop, dancing down the street.

A cup of tea? What do you mean?
It's coffee here; it's all in the bean.
Coffee, coffee everywhere—table, chair, couch, and floor.
It's time to leave out the door.

We'll be back for a cup of brew,
maybe a slice of cake—or make it two.
See you soon, my coffee mate.
Coffee, coffee, coffee—
it tastes so great.

I Had a Dog Called Chocky

I used to have a dog called Chocky.
He was as mean as a dog could be—
most of the time, *some* of the time to me.

He would eat the socks right off my feet,
eat just about anything found off the street.
Cats, birds, balls he would munch.
Dogs sure are a wild, wild bunch.

Oh, Chocky, why did you eat my socky?
Now you have to see the docky
because of the socks you ate right off my feet.
Oh, Chocky, why don't you eat pedigree meat
instead of the socks off my feet?

Oh, Chocky, oh, Chocky, that's my boy, Chocky.
Can't be mad at you now.
I hope he doesn't try to eat a cow.
I can laugh about it all now,
my mad dog called Chocky.
(10 April 2018)

Ghostly Ghouls

Ghostly ghouls fly through the air
to frighten me out of my underwear.
They're on my roof, tap, tap, tapping through the night.

Oh, my good God, please turn on the light!
Night-time comes, night-time goes.
Why now is it going so slow?
Ghostly ghouls leave signs of goo
on the window ledge; they are almost through!

They come with creepy stuff in their hands,
like skulls, insects, eyes, and bits of rubber bands.
The smell of death is in the air.
No wait, it's me and my underwear!

Time to run out to somewhere safe.
Oops, I realise I can't move now; I am far too scared.
I should have gotten myself prepared.

Time to push on till morning.
Noises around me are like sounds of ghouls groaning.
Monsters are in pain, or do they cause the noise that keeps me up all night,
keeps me still under bedcovers so tight?

Daytime comes just in time.
All's OK now; the day is all mine.
But you never know—they might still be there
to frighten me out of my underwear.

Green and Brown

Why is nature so green and brown,
slow as it grows, growing up and down?
Frown, frown, green and brown.
Nature's gone up and underground.

Bugs come throughout the year;
flies, bees, and wasps fly about your ear.
Bees come to pollinate your plants.
Drunk on pollen, watch them rant,
buzzing here, buzzing there.
Watch out! They are everywhere!

Flowers bloom, white-yellow to red;
turning to orange, now leaves fall around your head.
Smells of autumn in the air,
conkers, conkers everywhere.
Halloween cool and warm days at rest,
somehow autumn's the best.

Trees' orange-yellow-red leaves, ore for your eyes.
Time's a limit; trees' leaves fall down, fly by.
Cool wet winds, November's on its way.
Time for garden storage, put all away.

Jingle, jingle, white all night.
Frosty berry keeps us warm and merry,
reminds us of colours red and cherry.

One year over, now colours come back 'round.
Why is nature so green and brown?
Maybe I'll find out in the year ahead.
Seeing colour all around, it's gone to my head.
Staying in my garden bed of green and brown,
no need to frown: It's all green and brown.

Music to My Feet, or Joy Doing a Jay

I nearly got arrested the other day on the boulevard, a street around my way.
I had my dinner in my arms; I could not do any harm,
so the fuzz let me go on my way.
I could not believe my luck;
it would have made my night really suck.
Got sent on my way, but it could have gone the other way.

Saved by my burger and chips!
The police were giving me lip, nearly dropped my chips.
You should have seen me there on the boulevard,
trying to act so hard with my dinner in my hand.
I wish I looked so grand with my dinner in my hand.

Brought with my Visa card, I got a can of drink for free,
like me; I was set free on the boulevard after stopped by police.
Oh, what a sweet release!

To taste my dinner in peace, nearly got arrested by the police,
then left alone by the police.
I can understand why because I had to walk on by
a dual carriage way down my way.
On the boulevard, pulled over for doing a jay.
"Jaywalking", they say.
What a serious crime at that time. They say,
"Lucky boy, could have gone the other way."

Working for Molly

Oh, Molly, you make me work so hard.
Molly, you are a witch, ohh, Molly, oh, Molly.
You pay me in pennies which has given me a nervous twitch.
I have blisters on my fingers and sores on my feet.
Been working so hard forever, now just to fall at your feet.

Take me, let me lie at your side.
I have had enough of you and your lies.
These blisters make my feet so sore.
I know I have to head for the door.
I need new shoes or to get rid of you.
You have left me with not much to do.

Finally got out that door to never look back; you left me so poor.
Maybe I will smash your foot in the door
to leave you in pain,
feet swelling in pain again and again.
Oh, Molly, oh, Molly, finally on your own, Molly.
No one's calling you on your phone
Oh, Molly, oh, Molly.

Now I'm back home, feeling so much better.
Blisters healed, and money's looking better.
Never coming to see you, Molly, never.

Nationwide How We try'd

nationwide i hope you'r proud of your self
a life you stole like from the shelve
men you took advantage of
you should of helped, not then you shoved

a man's life waiting in vain
to reduce the arrears all ways left in pain
year after year to kind to let you down
that's the man who's arrears wont go down
hard works what makes a man
nationwide must have had a plan
too keep the balance far too high
our father's life flew right by

see him work two, three,jobs at once
must have been mad running around like a ponnce
money money come and go you see
said give me money give it all to me

nationwide i hope you are proud of your self
that man has now fallen from that shelve
given up on life in his final beat
nearly lost his life working on his feet

must be man's fault going after the life
or was it your's ucb, you provided the strife
never letting up on interest, interest must be paid
forever father now he's to be laid
rest my father the deed's been done

i'll show them what is to be done
no more life's taken in vain
interest interest it drives you insane

it's too late now house price's now far to far out of reach
we was told we was all ways in the breach
contract contract, tear up waste of time
it has ruined future jobs have to wait in a long line
nationwide has caused all the mess
given May and boris stress stress stress
going to take time to sort the mess,
buy a caravan and you get less stress

bankers ban all bankers they are never thankers
by Christopher t knight
Chris t knight

The Pie Song

I went to my local shop, but I didn't know what to buy.
You see, I ended up with this girl by my side when I helped her pick a pie, yes, pie.
She couldn't decide which to buy.
I had to be fast on my feet to meet this girl, standing beside the frozen meat.

I couldn't believe my luck when she glanced over to look.
You know, we were going to book a date next week
because of that pie, that pie I helped her pick.
Now I might be in so quick; pie, yes pie, the pie I helped her pick.

So we left the shop with a couple of pies.
Back home for a dinner date; Mum, you know I am going to be late.
You may as well put my dinner in the oven on a plate.
Yes pie, pie, the pie I helped her pick.

So don't forget to shop.
You never know what you might find
in those corner shops down your way; go get them, guys.
Girls love them meat pies, the one I helped pick

Because of those pies, I now have a girl by my side.
Now I love to shop at my local paper shop.
You know, where I'll be down the aisle, making girls smile.
And helping to pick those pies, the ones girls love to pick.

Play the Lottery

When my life goes to shit, can't help myself, it seems to be
I head to the shops to play the lottery.
All the numbers in front of me,
must be the fun and monotony in playing the lottery.

My life has gone to shit; I have gotten caught in a rut.
It makes me feel like I want to kick someone's butt.
Life's gone to shit; it seems to last for ages.
Nothing around my life ever changes.

It seems like fun up at the till,
paying for those numbers; oh, no, now I am gonna be ill.
Walk out feeling sick; I have just spent a fortune on numbers.
What a twit!
Luck has run out; it comes and goes.

Must be the monotony of the lottery, see how the jackpot grows.
I can't win; I have bad luck.
See, I nearly stepped in that dog muck.
At home, now lottery's on the box.
Hope and pray I haven't just lost the lot.

The balls are in the spinning drum.
I hope and pray my new life is yet to come.
What to do with the dough once I win?
Sod it, the tickets are in the bin.
No numbers; once again, the lottery brings me much more pain.
You know I will try again and again,
wasting my money all down the drain.

Must be the monotony of the lottery.
The lottery monotony has gotten to me.
Play the lottery; it's all monotony.

SES Meeting Time and Place

I met a girl called Mandy some time ago.
She told me things I should need to know.
Some things about things called a show.
I didn't know at the time which way to go.

She put me in the orange and green
to try to keep the streets safe and clean.
SES, you must know what I mean.
Kind of late, but I always made it on time.
Shumaccer Mandy, a good team, became a good friend of mine.
Met a girl called Mandy; she's on the road, M1.
Missed the exit; oh, well, try to have some fun.

SES times have begun, never late, position on the gate.
Position's safe, now that's the way.
Mandy, Mandy, look out the way you drive us all every day.
Mandy, Mandy, there's no other way; then a roundabout got in the way.
Mandy, Mandy, always on the ball,
never seems to slip and fall.
Great days in the sun, wind, and rain,
I want to work again and again.
Health and safety hazards, stay on the ball; some customer act like fools.
In the sun's heat, try to keep your cool.
Running hot, try to catch the sun.
When with SES, it seems to mean having fun.
Sunburnt head? Use plenty of cream.
I'm looking like a tomato; I think I should have used salad cream.
Job's done, now on the way home.
Some start to moan and groan.
Soon we will be back on the phone.
Next job isn't too far away.
Mandy, Mandy, stay safe the SES way.
Sometimes it was loud, told us how to control a crowd,
people packed in like sardines in the pit.
Crowd's safe, now see you in a bit.
Team SES, we have all done well; Joe, Ian, Shaid, Ben, and Dee,
too many to mention I have met this year, you see.

My Girlfriend Rebecca

I got a girl called rebecca
I feel I could do no better
kind of girl who would knitt me a sweater
time we spent together, "never better"
oh rebecca I do love the sweater

out of the blue things started turning blue
yer she even threw my shoes
things were all most great
now she has chucked my cloths over the garden gate

why rebecca why rebecca
never did you wrong rebecca
two dogs house together it's all gone wrong rebecca
tell me whats wrong rebecca

turns out she hates my ways, my habbits are turning her away
now what am I to do, you have ruined my fav shoe's
you have turned my mood
just my nervious twitch getting on your nerves
man what a nervios twitch
and the way I sniff and blow my nose
should of stayed away I suppose

so I have left her now and took the sweater
moved on to somthing better
maybe I will sell the sweater arrrgh rebecca
no, now ive have pissed on the sweater
arrrghhhh now I feel better.

Christopher knight

Printed in the United States
by Baker & Taylor Publisher Services